Negative Thinking:

Easy Guide To Believe That Everything Is Awesome!

Disclamer: All photos used in this book, including the cover photo were made available under a <u>Attribution-NonCommercial-ShareAlike 2.0 Generic</u> and sourced from <u>Flickr</u>

Table of content

Introduction

In scenarios that it gets difficult to self- talk the right path out of negative thoughts, you will must relax your mind. Begin to breathe gradually and deeply to obtain more oxygen into your brain to assist you think greater and calm yourself from hyperventilation. Think about issues that will help you clean out negative thoughts once you have calmed down. Like, "what's the best thing todo?" should you experience difficulties that are situational. Wondering questions that can make a situation is acted upon by you will likely make you do things to take care of that certain scenario.

Since bad thinking upsets the way you accomplish, make sure to have a service process. People, who you'll be able to run to in times of mischief and question, will help you exceed your dilemma. They're able to give tips that you can think about to you. They are able to even encourage you to feel absolutely. Choosing the visitors that are right to convert to is not unimportant. That person have to be trusted and recognize you effectively to ensure that you can be reassured that he or she'll really help you.

Dealing with cure unfavorable thinking is easier said than done. You may want to consult anyone to counsel you if you think that your event gets worse. Counselling can help you realize the main reason which you assume how you do. A counsellor might even allow you to cure unfavorable thinking through cognitive renovation or cognitive behavioral therapy.

Chapter 1 – How negative thinking destroys your life

The mental poison begin to slide into our mind when we're sensation reduced or down on confidence. You're upset that your colleague got a which you didn't. Or you got dumped even if you had been trying to function as the finest companion on the planet.

While everyone be seemingly getting the time of their life and the toughest part, you have no idea why you're usually the one who has to undergo via a poor life. If you're an energetic Facebook individual with a huge selection of pals online, you're bound to view plenty of content images and vacation snapshots on a regular basis. It sucks, doesn't it? You're cooped at home all-day while friends and family revise every moment of their effective, fun lives. Happier than you!

And right-about there, you begin to make details and explanations up for that boredom and distress that you experienced. As opposed to realizing that half your web pals simply share these smiley -faced images and constant changes with the whole world only to feel a lot better about themselves and their lifestyles that are vacant, you assume that you're the depressing one who's got nothing to not become unhappy about. Bad thinking could be the biggest difficulty in your endeavors as well as your life. And if you don't retain a check into it, you may find yourself feeling just like a failure all of your life.

How to stop thinking negative

Don't reside in denial. Attempt to remove the pessimism by examining the situation better if you've ever felt like you're a negative thinker. Lifestyle doesn't always have answers that are straightforward. If you would like to avoid imagining adverse, here are 10 typical instances of negativity and approaches to defeat them. Consider these cases and ask yourself how you'd react once you experience them. And when you feel like you're an adverse thinker, do something about it.

1 You often think the worst. When they're meeting up, friends and family forget to call you, you feel they're avoiding you. Your friends forget your birthday; you think they dislike you. A buddy pushes simply because they didn't discover you, without waving a hello, and you believe. Some people always suppose the toughest possible answers for anything. Maybe, at-times your thoughts are precise, however not constantly. Subtly mention the nagging thought should anyone ever feel terrible about anything and speak about it using the person that is involved. Assumptions that are making won't allow you to.

2 You never think from another perception that is person's. You imagine someone's treating you badly. Or you think your companion doesn't love you enough. Or you think your work is appreciated by your boss doesn't around your colleague's work. By what you aren't finding as opposed to crying, placed oneself within their shoes and attempt to understand why they respond how they do. Could you notice their aspect of the story to comprehend their purpose? Probably, you've several defects that you simply don't know however. Often assume from you'll and the different person's viewpoint turn into a better person with time.

3 You consider the entire world is unjust for your requirements. You obtain the toughest deals in life. You imagine you're the prey. Can you actually feel like regardless of what you need to do or challenging you attempt, you can never flourish in your efforts? Mark Zuckerberg's everything's and so damn wealthy really easy for him, isn't it? You function as the one with all the current sensible tips? Living isn't easy. But life's fair for the ones who are excited about it. You'll get where you want to move sometime in case you genuinely feel you're a lot better than everyone else. But at the same moment, possibly there's a little possibility that you're not-as good when you think you are. End playing the area of the prey and head out there and pursue your desire.

4 you're feeling like you can't rely on everyone. Are you some of those those who doubt everybody? You're a perfectionist just like you can't be determined by anyone if you feel. Or confidence is shouldn't be by someone others that are you're. Sometimes, the way we approach life affects the way we examine others. It is likely that, if you think you can't be respected, you won't learn to trust others too. In life, you have to trust some people and figure out how to rely on them. It will help you think in people that issue, and from your life, it eliminates uncertainty and pessimism at the same period.

5 you anticipate a lot of from everyone. You might not realize this, but you may assume the entire world revolves around you, and when others don't treat you the way in which you need them to deal with you, you feel dejected. Can you expect out when you're in a mess constantly others to help you? You're bound to feel bad when people don't go out of their solution to allow you to if you continuously rely on people for all your achievements. Dad and your mom may always be there to give you require to you. Nevertheless the world doesn't treatment. Learn create

your own personal successes and to remain true by yourself feet.

#6 You can't accept failure. In case you can't make a move or obtain your objective, it's too hard. And if other people does it, they got lucky. Have you ever felt by doing this? You're not alone. The world is filled up with people who can't accept it when their buddies become less unsuccessful. Prevent bringing luck into the situation of lifestyle, or you'll generally find yourself considering negative about everyone who defines anything you don't.

7 you merely have bad thoughts. You keep count of all adverse items that happen to you. Nevertheless you never remember the great items that you experienced. Life is full of moments. But when you discover oneself surrounded by the terrible moments of living as well as mental poison, you'll get enveloped in despair and gloom. Make an effort to consider things' shiny side and enjoy happiness' tiny minutes which come your way all the time. Negativity is contagious. They'll stressed around you too and experience adverse if you feel bad around people. Satisfied people will start to avoid you. And you'll begin to attract those who feel like you, not affirmative. Just like only friends and family know how depressing and illegal existence is can you feel? Odds are , surrounded by bad people.

9 friends and family laugh at you. You assume your pals are giggling at you, never. Can you feel like your pals are currently sniggering behind your back? Maybe you need friends if it's accurate. But if it's merely paranoia that is adverse, quit that. The planet maybe mean, but treat you horribly or that doesn't mean everyone's out there to poke fun at you. Probably, you're simply attempting to seek out anything terrible on a regular basis of how negative the planet is to you,

to tell yourself.

10 You're secretly very competitive. Does one react like a closest friend to everybody about, but deep inside, all you do is piece techniques for getting much better than them? Healthy competition is very good. But secretive overzealous planning never is. Do you get frustrated if a buddy buys a new automobile or perhaps a household? Would you attempt everything possible to buy the same thing just so you're able to experience also? In case you continually want to take on someone and be much better than them just to feel pleased about oneself, you're surviving in a shallow planet that'll often leave you annoyed negative and continually wanting more. Take on tomorrow and yourself, try to develop into an individual that is greater than you are today. It'll help you accomplish your targets is likely to conditions. Normally, nothing you have because you're consistently peeping over your neighbor's barrier is cherished by you'll.

Chapter 2 – Words You Need To Stop Saying About Yourself Right Now!

1. "I'm not adequate enough yet."

In the event you keep trying it might seem you're not good enough surprise yourself. Your past does not decide who you are. Your past makes you for who you're able to getting. What ultimately describes you is how well you increase after slipping. Don't ever be afraid to give oneself to be able to be everything you are designed for being. Forget the haters. Never undervalue what you're with the capacity of and who you're. Superiority is the consequence of loving over others believe is necessary, dreaming over others think is realistic, risking greater than others believe is secure, and performing greater than others think can be done.

2. "I should be living around different people's expectations."

Remember, it's usually safer to be at the ladder's underside you would like to rise compared to the surface of the one you don't. Delight and accomplishment is focused on investing your lifetime is likely to approach. Continually be oneself and wander your personal way. No-one can actually tell you you're doing it wrong. Everyone has a unique path that produces sense for them, their very own struggles, as well as their own goals. You're YOU to get a purpose.

If you find yourself living a dull, dismal life because you ignored oneself and rather heard a guardian, a tutor, or some gal on TV telling you how to live life, then you have no one-but yourself to blame. Just remember, pay attention to you and most and the best brave act is just to think yourself possess intuition. In the end, then live someone else's idea of your daily life it's better to die the right path.

3. "What they believe and say about me matters."

If you believed nobody could assess you, what could you do? Don't let others break your dreams. Do exactly once the things they say you can't do, and you may never pay attention to their negativity again. Don't leave from these adverse people... WORK! Whenever you distance yourself from those who generate it and negativity, nutrients happen.

Honestly, nobody gets to determine you. they can't experience what you are currently getting through, although individuals may have seen your reports. Therefore forget what they say about you. Concentrate on the method that you do that which you know within your heart, and feel about yourself is suitable.

4. "I need identification for my steps to be worthwhile."

Do what you know is appropriate. Ethics does the right thing, it doesn't matter what if nobody's planning to understand not or whether you achieved it. Life often finds its balance. Don't expect you'll get whatever you give back. Don't expect reputation for each effort you produce. And don't expect your kindness to become immediately identified or your love to be understood by everybody you encounter.

What may seem like the correct move to make could also be the hardest thing you've actually done. Do it anyway. There is no effectiveness or satisfaction where there is betrayal of your personal goodwill. Constantly goal at full sincerity of phrases your views and manners. If it is wrong, don't do it. Don't repeat it, if it's wrong. Do what you do as you consider it's the right action to take. Do the proper point even if nobody is currently searching. Be among the individuals who produce a legitimate difference on the planet than you found it by leaving it a little better and much more wholesome.

5. "Late for me."

Don't let yesterday take your current. Don't decide yourself by your past... you don't stay there. Let develop go, and move ahead. As we get older and wiser, we begin to realize what we must leave behind and what we require. Sometimes walking away can be an advance. Occasionally a break out of your schedule is strictly things you need. You will feel forever stuck unless you make an effort to master anything beyond what you know.

Don't waste another minute lamenting what you did yesterday, and commence doing everything you need to do so you won't regret today what you did. It's not too late. It's just your inner worries lying for you like it's if you feel. But remember, fear doesn't exist anywhere except in your thoughts. You are stopped by It's difficult it's a catastrophe to let the lies of fear, although to follow your center.

6. "I must have all of it figured out."

Does the walker pick the path? Feel it or not the latter. Occasionally the greatest desires which come accurate would be the aspirations you never actually realized you'd. It's about open-minded pursuit. You will find no wrong turns in existence, only paths you didn't understand you're meant to walk. There is a constant could be particular what's nearby. Maybe it's everything, or maybe it's nothing. You keep getting one foot facing another, then one-day you look-back and understand you've climbed towards the very beautiful mountaintop's peak.

7. "I don't have enough to become constructive and grateful."

Some times you'll locate diamonds and all you'll see is coal some nights. Nevertheless, every day is just a wonderful possibility really impact the world around you, practice appreciation, and to study. Do not ask tolerance, but also although for immediate satisfaction in your life to accept your worries that are present. Do not require brilliance in most for previous mistakes to not be repeated by the intelligence, although you are doing. For more before stating, do not ask, "THANK YOU" for everything you have acquired.

And remember, everything in existence is temporary. Therefore if items are great, relish it. It won't last. If factors are not good, don't worry since it won't last either. Because lifestyle isn't strain-free at this time, doesn't imply you can't chuckle. Because something is worrying you, doesn't suggest you can't laugh. The secret is usually to be pleased when it is minimal when your mood is superior and stylish.

8. "My life should be free from discomfort." and more easy

Great troubles create life fascinating; overcoming them makes life meaningful. It's the way you deal with distress and disappointment that decides your degree of joy and achievement. Chuckle at your faults and learn from them. Scam about your problems and gather strength from their website. Have fun with the difficulties you experience after which conquer them.

Emotional discomfort in existence, when approved, failures and crests, rises in a number of waves. Each wave wipes an old coating of you away and deposits treasures you never likely to locate. Out goes inexperience, in comes recognition; out moves annoyance, in comes durability; out moves hatred, in comes kindness. No-one would say these dunes of mental knowledge are easy to trip, nevertheless the beat of psychological discomfort that you just learn how to endure while doing so is pure, beneficial and prevalent. The distress ultimately leaves healthier and you tougher than it found you.

9. "I can't forgive them."

Forgiveness is a guarantee. Once you reduce somebody you are creating a guarantee not to contain the unchangeable past against yourself that is current. Forgiveness doesn't imply what happened was not absolutely inexcusable, also it doesn't indicate that individual must be welcome in your lifetime. It therefore are ready to let it go and move ahead with your lifestyle, and basically means you've produced peace with all the discomfort.

Forgiveness has nothing with releasing a felony of their offense to do. It has everything regarding releasing oneself of being a victim – of the burden letting go of the pain and transforming yourself from prey to victor.

10. "I am alone."

You can't ensure it is through on your own. None people can. That's why, thank goodness, you are never as alone when you occasionally experience. A lot of folks are fighting the same actual struggle alongside you. You could experience alone sometimes, nevertheless, you are not in being alone, alone.

To lose sleep worrying about a loved one. To possess trouble selecting up oneself after someone lets you along. Because somebody didn't value you enough to keep, to feel rejected. To be reluctant to use anything fresh for concern you may crash. None of this means you're dysfunctional or weird. It only means that you will need a very little time recalibrate and to regroup yourself, and you're human.

Regardless of how embarrassed or pathetic you're feeling about your own personal condition, you can find others on the market exceptional same thoughts. "I am on their own, once you hear yourself say, " it's merely your brain attempting to sell you a lie. There's always a person who may relate solely to you. Maybe you can't immediately talk to them, nevertheless they are available, and that's all that's necessary to understand right now.

Next steps...

Easily eavesdropped on your self-talk, could I hear claims that empower pleasure, or statements that oppose it? Next time you decide to unclutter your life and cleanup your room, start with your intelligent space by cleaning out the old lies and damaging self-talk yourself is typically recited to by you.

Chapter 3 – How To Stop Others From Affecting You With Their Negative Thinking

Are you experiencing acquaintances or any friends that are bad? You'll realize they aren't probably the most satisfying people to be around if so. Adverse people might be true downers in any dialogue. No matter what you claim, they've a way of spinning points in an adverse path. Some damaging people could not be thus affirmative that it thinks draining only being around them.

I've handled a good share of unfavorable people in my life. Once I was in junior university, a college population of bad pupils and instructors fundamentally surrounded me. My college wasn't the most effective of the ton, so most people inside were dissatisfied by virtue of being there. Channel it into action and I ultimately discovered to control it, though I had been originally taken aback by negativity of the people.

Today, I take care of pessimism on-and-off in my private growth function, particularly when you'll find followers or training clients in hardship. Rather than be afflicted with damaging power that is others', I'm now able to consciously take care of it. Below, 9 suggestions to cope with negative people in your lifetime are shared with you by I'll:

1) Don't get into a disagreement
Among the most critical issues I learned is not to question with a bad person. A poor individual probably has isn't likely to alter that simply because of everything you said and quite staunch landscapes. What you may claim, he or she will find 10 different causes to backup his/her perspective. More pessimism will be simply

swirled into by the talk, and you pull down oneself in the process. You can give good reviews, and don't indulge further if anyone rebuts of supporting down without indicators.

2) Empathize together

Before, subsequently have somebody let you know to "relax", maybe you have been annoyed by anything? Did you feel? Did you relax as the person recommended or did you are feeling a lot more worked up?

From my experience, folks who are negative (or upset for instance) gain more from an empathetic ear than recommendations/options on which he or she have to do. By supporting them to deal with their thoughts, the options can quickly arrived at them (it's always been inside them anyway).

3) Lend a helping hand

Many people complain as an easy way of crying for support. They may unconscious of it however, thus their responses run into as claims in the place of requests. Take the responsibility to lend a helping hand. Merely a straightforward "Are you "Is or ok?" there something I - can do to assist you?" can perform wonders.

4) Follow light topics

Some folks that were negative are triggered by particular issues. Consider like: One-Of my buddies sinks in to a self-victimizing mode once we discuss his work. It doesn't matter what I say (or don't declare), he'll keep complaining even as we talk about function.

Your 1st impulse with bad people should be to help carry a more them constructive area (i.e. Methods Number 2 and Number 3). But if it's obvious anyone is trapped in his/her pessimism, the depression could be also deeply seated to address in a-one-off chat, or for you yourself to enable him/ it is unraveled by her. Bring in a brand new theme to reduce the feeling. Easy such things as fresh films, everyday incidents, buddies that are widespread, create for talk that is light. Preserve it to parts the person seems beneficial towards.

5) Disregard the adverse reviews

One method to enable the negative person "get it" is to disregard the negative responses. Dismiss or offer a simple "I see" or "Ok" response if she or he switches into a negative swirl. In excitement and report, when she or he is being beneficial, answer to the hand. Do that often and shortly he/she will realize positivity takes care of. He or she can adjust to be much more constructive appropriately.

6) Reward anyone for the good points

People that are adverse aren't merely negative to others. They're also damaging to themselves. Should you already experience not affirmative around them, envision how they need to experience constantly. What're the items the person is great at? What can you like concerning the person? Recognize praise and the constructive things him/ her. He/ she will be amazed at-first and may decline the compliment, but inside he/she'll feel good about it. That's planting in him primary seed / her and it'll bloom within the longterm.

7) Hangout with more people or 3's

Having somebody else while in the conversation works miracles in reducing force. In a 1-1 transmission, all the pessimism will be directed closer. With another person within the discussion, you don't need to carry the total brunt of the negativity. This way it is possible to target more on performing measures #1

(Empathizing and Number 2 (Assisting anyone).

8) Result in your reaction

Perhaps the individual is negative or not, fundamentally you're the one who is perceiving the individual is damaging. Whenever you observe that, truly the negativity will be one's lens' merchandise. Take responsibility for the perceptions. In a negative approach and a confident, it is possible to read it for every single feature. Learn to see the person's goodness as opposed to negative. It may not be tender originally, but it becomes second nature once you enhance the expertise.

9) Minimize experience of them/prevent them

Lower connection with them if all else fails or prevent them altogether. Allow him if it's an excellent buddy /her understand of the issue's intensity and function it out where feasible. It's not healthy to pay too much time with individuals who strain you. Your time and effort is important, thus spend it with people who have results you.

Chapter 4 – 7 Simple Steps To Change Your Vector From Negative To Positive

There's room for every one of us and development in each, there's no such issue as being an individual that is great - though lovers of specified celebrities of the other gender and that declaration occasionally may disagree! No, if it were an earth that is perfect there will be rage no unhappiness, panic or faults. Nevertheless, it appears strange doesn't it that while excellence is an ideal we can never attain, through knowing our defects and striving to eradicate them, we are able to truly get nearer to excellence through our personal imperfection.

So, how do we accomplish that then? Well, it really is generally what we obviously do every day of our lives. We door attempt something, we-don't get it very right therefore we analyze what occurred, work-out what we have to complete to stop that happening again and what went not correct and then try. This time then happy days, if we do it right! If not, we replicate the method. That investigation process might simply take a minute for the brains to procedure, such could be the amazing power of the mind it is basically our personal super-computer.

Learning from your own faults.

That procedure we simply talked about is the greatest understanding method there is. Whichever it is in life you might like to do, only do it. Create your errors, fix them-and try again. Soon you are going to go out of faults to make. Because the people that caused it to be wonderful had ambitions which they produced authentic, we live in a beautiful world. Nevertheless, they didn't succeed in the first test, oh no, there have been some very stunning problems as you go along nevertheless the stage is at how they do things, they looked, exercised what problems they fixed them, made and attempted again. That is all that's necessary to complete to start out generating positives out of your problems.

What is stopping you?

Well it is the fear of making errors, of what other people might believe or door claim about them that prevents them from seeking different things. Don't allow this be you. Do not spend your time house on what may occur if you crash rather than the possible gains that may come the right path in case you succeed. This kind of bad thinking is what you would like to eliminate, it might become while the mental poison carry forth a variety of bad photographs as opposed to the constructive people you intend to be making, paralyzing. This attitude that is negative will root one to the spot, you will commence to see mistakes as insurmountable problems in the place of learning options.

Therefore, now that your mindset has now reached that milestone, start powering up on your own- self and perception confidence. Put to function, by getting the views to movement from adverse to optimistic produce the power. Study from proceed and your faults upward and onward.

Here are 4 steps to earn using a good attitude.

1. Implement and it is not too early to understand constructive perspective tips? No it's too early use and to learn recommendations that allow you to maintain your attitude beneficial. Like a matter-of-fact the earlier you figure out how to manage your attitude and maintain it an optimistic one you will benefit in most aspects of your lifetime from it.

2. Can I truly see benefits from positive perspective methods? Yes, you will really observe results that are rapid and you will quickly note that you're getting more completed and looking towards every part of living. This is one of many simplest activities to do for yourself if it is damaging and it really just takes time to check in with oneself and see where your attitude is. Then only create a positive selection to make your perspective maintain positivity. When you do that simply keep tracking it to help yourself keep it there

3. Who must use optimistic perspective tips? Everybody must employ these attitude tips to create their lifestyle of better quality and entertainment. Then decide to keep your perspective optimistic in case you genuinely wish to live a great and happy living packed with laughter and love which is what you will encounter.

4. How fast could I observe result with good perspective recommendations? from using positive perspective recommendations, you can observe immediate derive. If you simply enable them to meet your needs. That is merely an issue of maintaining an open mind and select the outcome of every day by thinking favorably about everything you do. Should you make this a normal practice to become around good people in positive environment? Also you wish to allow yourself to keep tuned and concentrated to the good things in life that you just do desire in existence. You can start reading and hearing positive upbeat learning material about perceptions and how they result you. Look for an advisor that can help coach you if you feel that's what you may need initially to get your attitude encouraging and more constructive. Should you choose these few points for yourself? Then you will certainly begin enjoying today yourself starting right now.

Positive Attitude Tips: Here what's in this essay that I published simply for you.

* Are Attitude tips only baby stuff?

* Are good attitude methods really consequence?

Have you ever been around someone who is always negative about everything? It is adequate to drive you crazy. But more importantly have you ever be described as an individual that is negative? If you answered yes to the above concern then browse the methods that I published just for you. If you utilize them, you will be pleasantly shock in the difference that is positive it might produce in your life.

Here are 2 Key Suggestions To Keeping a Positive Attitude.

Are Attitude guidelines simply kid stuff? Constructive attitude methods aren't just kid stuff. Your perspective effects everything in your life. I am unable to show to you personally that learning how to have a superior perspective in life is perhaps among the top items that can bring success and continued happiness within your everyday life to you.

Are optimistic perspective methods definitely result? Yes, on how-to have a superior attitude if learned and applied properly on a frequent schedule tips can be extremely able to working for you get excellent results. Because your attitude comes with an impact on the outcome of each matter that you just every do. It's not unimportant to keep it positive that way if you have an optimistic mindset it helps to start your mind to understand and take available on the tasks. It will help you to complete all you do more simply. In which a bad perspective steals your time because you're needing to fight to be able to get something accomplished to overcome your negative attitude and by the period and attracts you down you do this you're drained of the valuable energy inside you.

You intend to begin checking your attitude of course if you will find that it's negative on changing it into a positive attitude then focus. By assisting the mind to target on the consequence that you simply do want not about what you don't want you're able to best try this. Likewise, should you learn how to be grateful for the items that are great that you've in your lifetime like you're a healthy body, food to eat, apparel to wear along with a roof over your head. The capacity to communicate and be observed these things all, your reading, your perspective will allow you to possess a more beneficial outlook on lifestyle.

Chapter 5 – Daily Exercises To Strengthen Your Positive Thinking

You are being weighed by fed up with sensation like the planet along? If you're battling to change how you perceive the world around you, it's moment that you begin on some helpful constructive thinking exercises. Reports show that people who have a confident perspective towards living are not information and simply happier about their lifestyles, but they may also be ready to handle challenges in a healthier fashion. Optimistic attitude activities won't simply enhance your total mood, but also can allow you to enhance your daily life in ways that you simply never expect. Where bad thinking routines which lessen your power to enjoy a prosperous and for filling lifestyle and will store you back.

Positive Thinking Exercises Number 1 Open your Mind

Step one to creating a positive attitude is to open your mind to Thinking Activities and be more conscious of your surroundings. Figure out how to listen to other people sides and make an effort to understand where they're via. If you're also set on your own ways, there's an opportunity that you'll get trapped in your own opinion system and therefore, not be aware of different suggestions that surround you. Don't simply write off new suggestions just because they look too farfetched or impossible to reach. With the open mind, you'll start to observe that you'll find unlimited options before you.

Positive Thinking Exercises Number 2 Record down 10 Points you're Happy for Everyday

Another straightforward solution to possess a good head through positive-thinking exercises is by detailing down at least 10 items that you're pleased for each day. Developing a good view is not something that will just come naturally overnight. It needs continual practice thus it's critical that discover occasion for this task every day. You don't always need to record massive and over the top factors, since even the littlest things may suffice. Whether it's a sunny evening, or perhaps a shock cake produced by someone you care about, having something to be grateful for might help you transform the manner in which you view oneself and your life total.

Positive Thinking Exercises Number 3 Learn How To Reflect Daily

Last however, not the least, ensure that you discover time to meditate daily. Yoga is definitely some efficient methods to not merely obvious your mind of pessimism, but also be described as a means for one to feel better physically. You don't have to be a religious person in order to meditate. It's as simple as finding a quiet place where you are able to do some quiet thinking yourself. If you're a morning person, start your yoga period by taking a peaceful long walk before everybody else awakes. If you're a night person on the other-hand, you may also reflect by relaxing in a peaceful space, free of distractions and you should be alone with your views. After you obtain the hang of meditating daily, you'll become more in-tune with oneself and be more available to good thinking. You'll find numerous relaxation methods as you are able to use. It's only a matter of finding the right one for you.

As a way to efficiently pull-off these positive thinking exercises, it's essential that you free oneself from inhibiting views and suggestions. Set your sights towards a more beneficial lifestyle and you'll feel just like a whole new individual right away. Use these Positive-Thinking Techniques to raise your self-esteem and start living you imagined.

Positive Thinking Exercises No 4 Self-Esteem Exercises

Nobody is ideal. As there are flaws there are the maximum amount of positive characteristics in us. Give attention to what you cultivate it can do properly and allow it to be part of your daily. By contemplating your errors, you will be held back. Simply does it now — so what should you fail? Problems improve you. At yourself will be the stronger you feel, the higher how you look. Make use of the subsequent affirmations and see how your self-confidence rockets.

Our self-esteem increases everyday

I take all facets of myself

I believe positive feelings of myself

I'm confident in myself

I've endless confidence in myself

I am limitless in my skills

I will do anything

Our self-esteem is hardly low

Our self-esteem is unlimited

Anything I need is attained by me

When I am I recognize myself

I love myself when I am

I believe in myself

I understand who I am

I know my skills

I speak favorably of myself

Much like physical activity, daily practice is required by these psychological/ psychological workouts till they become automatic. Once they're automatic, you'll experience a remarkable change within your joy and you'll start to see the nice things arriving at you quite, very quickly.

1. Say no to mental poison. Help it become a spot every day to restore negative thoughts with constructive thoughts. Say NO to these ideas if you discover oneself within the throes of negativity and change them with emotional images of that which you desire in that condition.

2. Surround yourself with people that are content!2. Surround yourself with people that are happy. Avoid people who are jaded, depressed, bad, poisonous, furious, essential, judgmental and stunning. Like attracts like! Surround yourself with positivity adopt it as the right path of being very swiftly, and too at that! It seems GOOD to not be neutral!

3. Be happy. This can be the positivity workout that is strongest that is single! Offer thanks for anything in your life, like trials, worries, challenges and the difficulties. That includes the folks who cause you to upset and frustrated. to what the silver coating and the blessing might be in most situation give critical considered. If you enable oneself to determine if there IS one! Give thanks for everything you have, and for what you need to have. Consider carefully your living in terms of what's wonderful, not what's missing. As mirrors – there is something within their conduct that mirrors some notion you keep, even though it's difficult to acknowledge that see tough people.

4. Be considered a Yes/Grin Collector. Have a great time obtaining "yeses" and smile every day. You realize laughs are infectious and they're immediate mood-lifters. Do what you can to generate people smile at you and state "yes" for your requirements more regularly – present to aid, make a move random and form, work, talk constructive terms, let them have one among your absolute best laughs

5. Meditate. You can certainly do a wonderful positive relaxation should you focus on delivering out love to everybody you know (again, like the tough and annoying people!). Label them by one off one, and state and feel love you" in their mind. You'll be shocked at how easily you burn into that love, and the way excellent it seems! Relaxation is a great time to let go of your tension. A regular practice has many benefits that are physical, emotional, intellectual and spiritual.

6. Fake it 'til you make it. Sometimes, it's nearly impossible to not experience neutral. PRACTICALLY. Thus wear a happy-face – LOOK! Before the concept out of your facial muscles gets through to your mind – and you start to feel happier. Such as helping others doing positive things can snap you from a funk. Even though you don't if there's no sun and feel just like it, get right up, get outside in to the sunshine –, create some with your own personal superb grin! Be grateful and learn to see the YES.

7. Do unto others. It's generally good to do great things for others; but particularly powerful and ideal for you should you put your personal challenges aside and give attention to helping others. Volunteer at the homeless shelter or a dog shelter; commit each day offering unwanted objects and cleaning out your garage; offer to aid a neighbor using their project; invest some time at a senior middle. Do whichever enable you to feel useful good and beneficial!

8. Learn to see the Yes. Utilize your creativity to find out a possible good outcome in the place of a potential unfavorable consequence. The near future is inside your hands! Creatively imagine what you would like, and maintain that mental impression until it feels normal and right. Practice... that has an enormous payoff is taken by this!

Positive thinking can be a choice. A life- decision that is altering. Make use of the Love to master how-to boost your vibration that is positive. Then view your daily life change inside the most methods that are wonderful!

Conclusion

Negative thoughts can and can damage your lifetime.

A head full of mental poison makes you your life miserable.

You may feel along.

You lose confidence.

You don't think you are going to succeed.

You stop trying.

The incorrect options are made by you.

You beat up yourself.

You try to succeed and try.

But those mental poison quit you.

They bombard you with a you can't do that perspective till it pushes one to give up.

With all those negative thoughts you'll result in debt as well as in detrimental or damaging relationships or you'll get complacent in the present scenario you are in and won't desire to improve. Understand it is your birthright to not become scarce.

If you would like to achieve success, enjoy more happiness, more prosperity, inner peace and better associations then you certainly have to get rid of the negative thoughts and damaging beliefs.

Replace these bad feelings with constructive ideas that allow you enjoy and to succeed life.

By reading this eBook, you'll discover things that are various such as:

We all have negative thoughts.

As much as you attempt you won't unable to remove all your thinking that is negative.

Nevertheless, you may get rid of the continual mental poison.

You can get reduce the negative thoughts that destroy your lifetime.

It is possible to modify the bad values that reduce you from obtaining and succeeding your targets.